R.C. Gorman
The Posters

R.C. Gorman
The Posters

Introduction by Tricia Hurst

NORTHLAND PRESS  FLAGSTAFF, ARIZONA

FRONT COVER: *Santa Fe Woman*
BACK COVER: Original painting
by Rory Wagner

Copyright © 1980 by R. C. Gorman

All Rights Reserved
FIRST EDITION
ISBN 0-87358-221-7 (paper)
ISBN 0-87358-220-9 (cloth)
ISBN 0-87358-226-8 (limited)

Library of Congress Catalog Card Number 79-57397
Composed and Printed in the United States of America

INTRODUCTION

R. C. GORMAN, CONSIDERED BY MANY THE PREMIER artist among American Indians, is difficult to place in a neatly defined category. Gorman enjoys being the center of controversy as much as he enjoys being a Navajo. Many critics call him brilliant, the star of the Navajo Nation, a genius. Others call him arrogant, brash, flamboyant, aloof, and crazy. Most agree that his talent is universally outstanding.

His uninhibited, free-flowing style and vivid color sense are what catch and hold the eye. He has been called "the Picasso of American Indian artists," and his work is often compared with that of Raul Anguiano and Francisco Zuñiga.

Women predominate in his drawings; woman is the subject Gorman loves. Gorman says: "Women are a constant challenge because their infinite variety invites an infinitude of interpretations." For years he has been painting a portrait of the enduring Navajo woman — an earthy, stoic, nurturing, enigmatic woman — unglamorous but beautiful. The women he paints give us an insight into his heritage, and the many facets of his Indian past emerge through the deft strokes of his brush, pen, and pencil. The racial memory of the man flows, and the woman is born.

Gorman works from live models. He says he draws energy from them. The model sets the mood. If she's sour, it shows. If she's spontaneous and alive, so is his work. Spontaneity is the keyword. If Gorman has to worry over a drawing, it won't be good. His best work can be done in a few short minutes, although he might return later and add a brush stroke or two. From these moments spring the Navajo woman as we have come to know her — nursing babies, picking corn, building fires, walking the desert, contemplating and occupying space softly and with a monumental fullness.

True sophistication is often simplicity, unadorned and uncompromised. These are the ingredients that Gorman unfailingly brings to his work, and this is what viewers sense in the bright and bold splashes of color, light, and form.

Articulate, intelligent, and a keen observer of the world in which he lives, Gorman has an uncanny gift for discarding all that is frivolous and extraneous, and going straight to the heart of the matter. This is apparent in both his painting and his private life. For example, his reticence in vocally sharing his Navajo experience: he has learned that his personal participation cannot be fully understood by others because they are coming by it secondhand. But here, in these posters, Gorman does with his talent what he declines to verbalize.

Born near Canyon de Chelly, in northeastern Arizona, on July 26, 1932, R. C. Gorman became a part of one of the Navajo reservation's more illustrious families. His great-grandfather, Peshlakai, a man of many talents, was considered one of the great leaders in Navajo history. He had been one of the survivors of the Long Walk in the winter of 1864, when the United States military forces herded the Navajo together and marched them more than three hundred miles to Fort Sumner. There they were imprisoned for four years, and hundreds died of cold, hunger, and disease. The Navajo were reduced to a quarter of their population before they were allowed to return to their home in Canyon de Chelly.

Peshlakai acted as a mediator between the United States government and his people, championed liberal attitudes toward education, and taught to his tribe the art of silversmithing he had learned at Fort Sumner. His influence dominated the Navajo more than that of any other man at the time, and it was the sale of the silver that helped them to survive.

This was the ancestry from which Gorman came. It was the people of his land who taught him the ways of his forebears, their strength, courage, and their struggle to retain their dignity. He learned well from them and, at an early age, began to show signs of following in the footsteps of his great-grandfather.

As a small child, using his hands or a stick, he made his first paintings with sand, rocks, and mud on the earthen floor of the hogan where he lived. In grade school he received his first recognition for his artistic endeavors: he drew a nude woman and was spanked by both his teacher and his mother. His stay in junior high school was brief: he was expelled. But in high school he became one of the top students in his class.

Toward the end of the Korean War, Gorman did a four-year hitch in the Navy and, while stationed in the Mariana Islands, ventured into his first and last attempt at commercial art. He earned a great deal of money painting pictures of the men's wives or girlfriends from photographs. Using a head and shoulder shot, he would copy it and draw a "pin-up" body underneath. He was an overnight success. In his usual democratic way, he charged the enlisted men two dollars and the officers seven!

His tour of duty enabled him to attend Guam Territorial College and whetted his appetite for more knowledge. He flew in an airplane for the first time and ate his first shrimp and artichoke. During these years Gorman realized that, as much as he loved his people and reservation, he could never return there to live with them. He had vast horizons to conquer.

In 1955, at the age of twenty-three, he enrolled at Northern Arizona University in Flagstaff, where he majored in literature and minored in art. The first scholarship ever given by the Navajo tribe was awarded him in 1958 to study outside the United States. Accepted at the College of Mexico, Mexico City, he was exposed for the first time to the works of the Mexican artists, Orozco, Tamayo, Rivera, and Siqueiros. Perhaps Gorman related to these artists because they had rediscovered the Indian in themselves. The impact of their creativity upon his thinking was monumental.

It was during these years that he found his style. He was also introduced to the medium of lithography, which has since become important to his work. He executed his first lithographs with master printer José Sanchez in Mexico City. After his studies in Mexico he moved to San Francisco. To supplement the meager income from his drawing, he joined the Models' Guild and became one of the most successful and popular male nude models.

Within a few short years, Gorman's name was listed among those whom far-seeing investors and collectors considered to be outstanding artists of the future. They have been proven to be correct. He has won countless awards, and his work is collected by discriminating private collectors and museums the world over. He was the only living Native American artist to be included in the show "Masterworks of the Museum of the American Indian," held at the Metropolitan Museum of Art in New York City. Two of his drawings were selected for the cover of the show's catalogue. He is the only living Indian artist in the Museum's permanent collection. He has also been honored by being the first artist chosen for a series of one-man exhibitions of contemporary Indian artists held at the Museum of the American Indian.

In 1979 he traveled to France to produce two original stone lithographs at the world-famous Mourlot Imprimeurs in Paris. Since 1852, Mourlot has made lithographs for Matisse, Bonnard, Utrillo, Leger, Picasso, and Dali. At the same time, the Musée Municipal de Saint-Paul in Saint-Paul de Vence, France, presented Gorman's first major European exhibition, with over twenty pieces of work shown. In New York City, the Damon Runyon-Walter Winchell Cancer Foundation honored him with a one-man exhibition at the Runyon-Winchell Gallery. In October 1980 he will return to Mourlot for further work in lithography, and there will be a one-man exhibition of his work at the Navajo Turquoise Gallery in Paris during the same month.

Gorman has gone through many phases in his canvas painting, each of them reflecting the cultural traditions of his Navajo heritage. The mediums he has mastered include etching, silk screening, sculpture, ceramics, and tapestry. About the posters *Apache Devil Dancer* and *Navajo Ceremonial Mask*, included in this book, he says, "The Indian art that people are enjoying now will soon be lost. Rugs, pottery, masks — all will disappear through integration. It's inevitable. It's sad."

The news media, both in the United States and abroad, have noted Gorman's meteoric rise in the art world, but it is his own special brand of mischievous humor and shenanigans that observers remember about him. Pictures in newspapers and magazines portray him perched on a camel in front of the pyramids in Egypt, standing in the pouring rain in Japan, or reclining nude on a couch in his studio — swathed in an Indian blanket, with an oversized brass rhinoceros lurking in the background. A recent full-page advertisement for his Navajo Gallery in both Taos and Albuquerque, New Mexico, depicts Gorman in a white Brooks Brothers suit, headband, and turquoise, clutching a giant tortilla. The caption reads, "You don't have to be Jewish to love the Navajo Gallery."

Raconteur, musician, writer, world traveler, connoisseur of fine wines and exotic foods, he can be found behind the wheel of his Mercedes-Benz, or in a plane, on his way to yet another opening of his works, where he autographs copies of books written about him. Doris Monthan's *R. C. Gorman: The Lithographs* presents the most indepth portrait of the man yet to be printed.

Gorman takes his current way of life in stride as he moves with grace among the international jet set; has his works collected by statesmen, industrialists, and such luminaries as Barry Goldwater, Andy Warhol, Gregory Peck, Erma Bombeck, Lee Marvin, Mr. and Mrs. Hal Wallis, and members of the DuPont family of Wilmington, Delaware; has his portrait painted by Andy Warhol; and dines with Vice-President and Mrs. Mondale. But Gorman has changed little. Of his presentation to Washington, D.C., society at the Mondales', he says: "I never got a chance to eat. They kept bringing plates and I would be asked a question. By the time I'd answered, someone would whisk the plate away! I remember the menu, though: cold loaf of veal. Great!"

In an interview on NBC's "Today" show, he began sculpting a head of his father, Carl, and asked on camera that a bit of brandy be supplied to warm his efforts. The Public Broadcasting Service documented his work, with Rod McKuen narrating. In an article in *People* magazine, Gorman dismissed his fame lightly, saying, "It's because of America's new awareness of itself. Before, everything was like cheese — imported."

He often thinks in terms of food, and a collection of his favorite recipes will appear soon in a new book, *Nudes and Foods: Gorman Goes Gourmet*. While Gorman amuses himself, he amuses others, and that's exactly how he intends it to be. He can't help it if he loves the pubs in London, the osso buco in Italy, the raw ham in Spain, and the calamari in Greece. He will also tell you that his favorite food is still the blood sausage his Aunt Mary Tsosie makes on the reservation.

In Taos, where he has made his home for the past eleven years, R. C. Gorman Day was proclaimed by New Mexico's governor. At a "roast" given by the Chamber of Commerce, packed to the walls by townspeople, his priest brought down the house when he said, "I'm not his confessor. I'm his psychiatrist, because he didn't like what the real ones were telling him." In his defense, his father Carl arose and replied, "He's always been a good boy." T-shirts were printed up for the occasion, and as one local writer put it: "A lot of artists could be featured in national magazines, but how many can walk into a restaurant and see the bartender sporting a T-shirt with their name on it?" This one read: "R. C. Gorman, Damn You, I Love You!"

This man from a hogan on the Navajo reservation in Arizona, who worked as a busboy at Grand Canyon, sorted mail in a post office, and "threw tomatoes around," is now one of the most controversial artists of his time. This he readily admits.

Gorman's philosophy is that one of the secrets of life is to treat all disasters as incidents and none of the incidents as disasters. "I've never stopped to bargain for happiness. My idea of a perfect person is one on whom nothing is wasted. I don't sit down and say I'm going to work, because nothing is really work unless you'd rather be doing something else. It just happens. I've been asked what I do when the models I've used for years grow older. I tell them my models don't age, they just get better. Maybe time has passed and something has happened to them, but it was a progressive and positive process."

R. C. Gorman is a man of today in every sense, yet his racial memory and much of his experience lie with the ancient ways and traditions of his people, with the cave paintings and petroglyphs that remain amid the ruins of the Anasazi in the land of the Navajo.

THE POSTER AS ART

Posters, or placards as they were once known, were designed to be posted in public places for the purposes of announcements and propaganda. Evidence of their use has been found in the ancient civilizations of Egypt, Babylonia, Greece, and Rome. Some of the wall paintings of Pompeii are clearly in the nature of announcements, and the Greeks posted notices in the marketplace and forum. Fifteenth-century churches used them as propaganda against the evils of sin, and playgoers of the eighteenth century kept theatre bills as mementos.

The invention of printing broadened the field and, in the 1790s, the lithographic process widened the technical possibilities of poster art. Not until 1845, however, did the poster as we know it today originate. At that time it was clearly in the form of an advertisement.

Both sides of the Civil War used posters to spread their messages. Probably one of the most famous and powerful posters of all time was the one used for American recruitment during World War I. A picture of Uncle Sam pointed a compelling finger at every passerby under a caption that declared, "Uncle Sam Wants You."

The elements of poster design are based on the idea that it must be visible at a distance and comprehended in one glance, so that lines are generally simple and colors few and bold. Lettering is kept at a minimum and the subject for illustration is usually striking.

Posters were already being designed by known artists in the seventeenth and eighteenth centuries. In the nineteenth century, Honoré Daumier, the French painter, cartoonist, and lithographer, made wide use of the medium. In the 1870s another Frenchman, Henri de Toulouse-Lautrec, made poster art almost synonymous with his name. With a biting, satiric quality, Toulouse-Lautrec depicted the music halls, circuses, and the people that frequented them in Paris at that time. But the poster did not attain its present position of respect until the last decade of the nineteenth century, after these artists had demonstrated its widespread effectiveness in new fields.

Among others who have followed in the footsteps of Daumier and Toulouse-Lautrec are Miró, Dufy, Matisse, Braque, Chagall, Manet, and Léger. Before his death, the prolific Pablo Picasso produced some 428 posters in connection with exhibits of his work and for charities, friends, and other interests. Within the last hundred years, illustrators who gained recognition as outstanding users of the poster medium include Aubrey Beardsley, Maxfield Parrish, Howard Chandler Christie, James Montgomery Flagg, Charles Dana Gibson, and Norman Rockwell.

The posters of R. C. Gorman will also pass into that time when the twentieth century is of the past and his Indian form, especially that of the Navajo woman, will come to represent a very special history of a lifestyle that once was and can never be again.

Of the ones included in this book he says: "I have different feelings about each and every poster I've completed. They bring back a mixture of emotions such as you might find if you picked up an old diary you had once written in and started turning the pages. For me, they bring the past into focus. Each poster is a part of the whole that is me." With only a few strokes of the pencil, all that is needed in a poster, Gorman produces masterful results in the technique, and that whole is completed.

With the advent of radio and television, the poster may have lost its original place as a commercial advertising medium, but as a form of graphic art it has come to stay. As a method of direct appeal it has yet to meet its master. In the world of art during the last fifty years, the poster has been collected and prized as a statement of the past. Today it is seen as an ongoing dialogue with the present. The number of collectors has mushroomed in the last few years, and museums and galleries throughout the United States and Europe now hang the poster along with the priceless oil canvas.

The dialogue of today will soon be a statement of the past, and one of the strongest visual bridges between the two will be the poster. R. C. Gorman will be remembered as the man who helped to build that bridge.

TRICIA HURST

R. C. Gorman

White Buffalo Gallery   Wichita, Kansas

WOMAN WITH PENDLETON BLANKET
1979   29 x 21 inches
White Buffalo Gallery, Wichita

MANY HORSES GALLERY

R.C. GORMAN 1979

740 N. LA CIENEGA BLVD • LOS ANGELES, CALIFORNIA 90069 • (213) 659-0737

RED BLANKET
1979   26 x 19 inches
Many Horses Gallery, Los Angeles

NAVAJO CEREMONIAL MASK
1975   23 x 18 inches
Museum of Navajo Ceremonial Art
(now the Wheelwright Museum), Santa Fe

R. C. GORMAN: The Lithographs
Millicent Rogers Museum 1978

YANABAH
1978   26 x 18 inches
Millicent Rogers Museum, Taos

SPIDER WOMAN
1976   24 x 18 inches
Dewey-Kofron Gallery, Santa Fe

WOMAN IN PINK BLOUSE
1979   21 x 15½ inches
Navajo Gallery, Old Town, Albuquerque

"Red Rug Motif" Acrylic on Canvas 48" x 42"

R.C. GORMAN

Paintings and Drawings   October 16-November 25, 1979

Bayard Gallery

RED RUG MOTIF
1979   27 x 20 inches
Bayard Gallery, New York City

WOMAN FROM CANYON DE CHELLY
1979   26 x 20 inches
Runyon-Winchell Gallery, New York City

57th Indian Market

SOUTHWESTERN ASSOCIATION ON INDIAN AFFAIRS, INC.

AUGUST 19 & 20 • SANTA FE, NM • PUEBLO INDIAN DANCES • PALACE PATIO • 3 & 4 PM

SANTA FE WOMAN
1978   27 x 21½ inches
Southwestern Association on Indian Affairs,
for the 57th Indian Market, Santa Fe

APACHE DEVIL DANCER
1977   30 x 24 inches
Santa Fe East Gallery, Austin

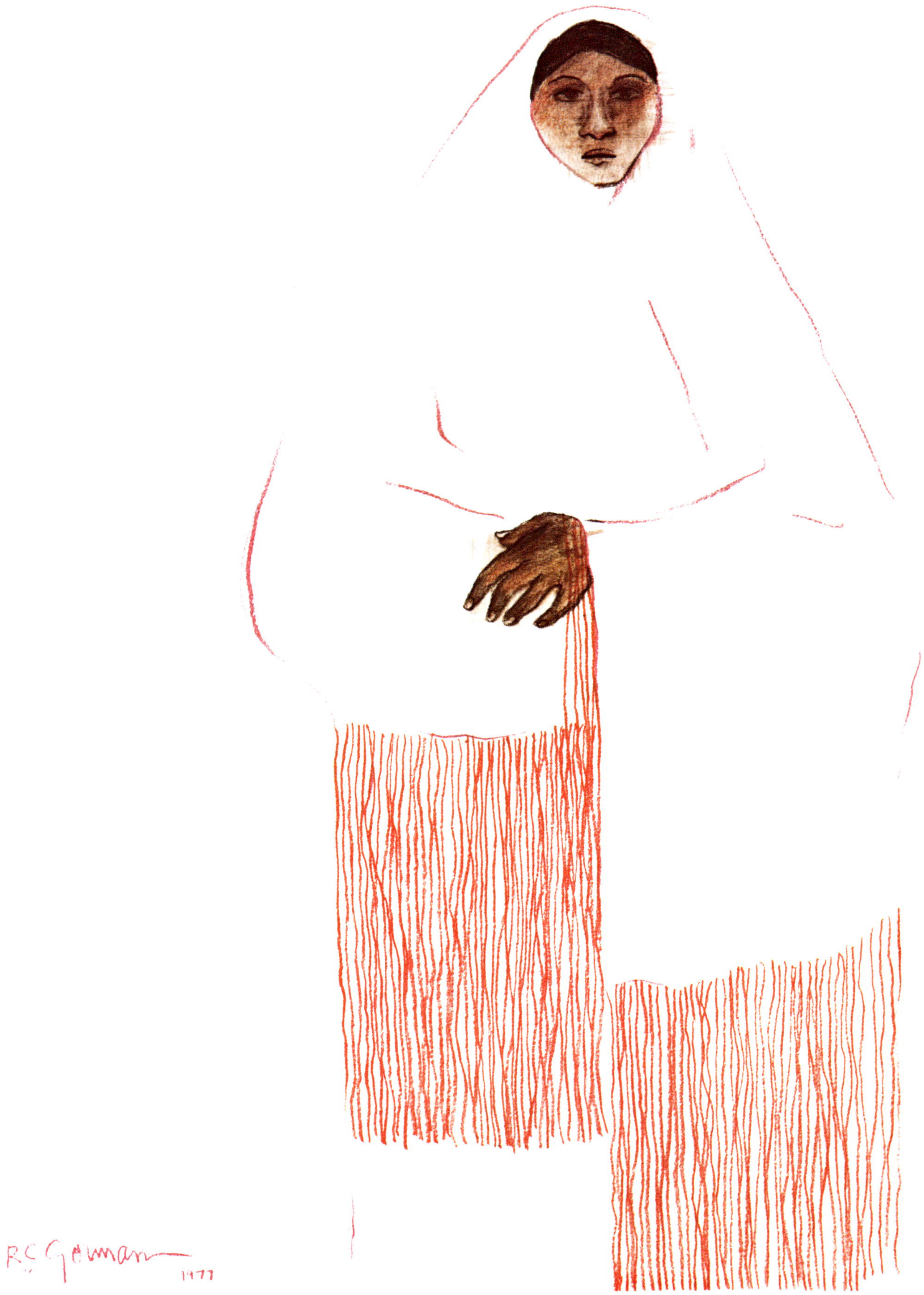

1977 R.C. GORMAN

TAOS PUEBLO WOMAN
1977   28 x 20 inches
White Buffalo Gallery, Wichita

Rutherford

A Working Lieutenant Governor

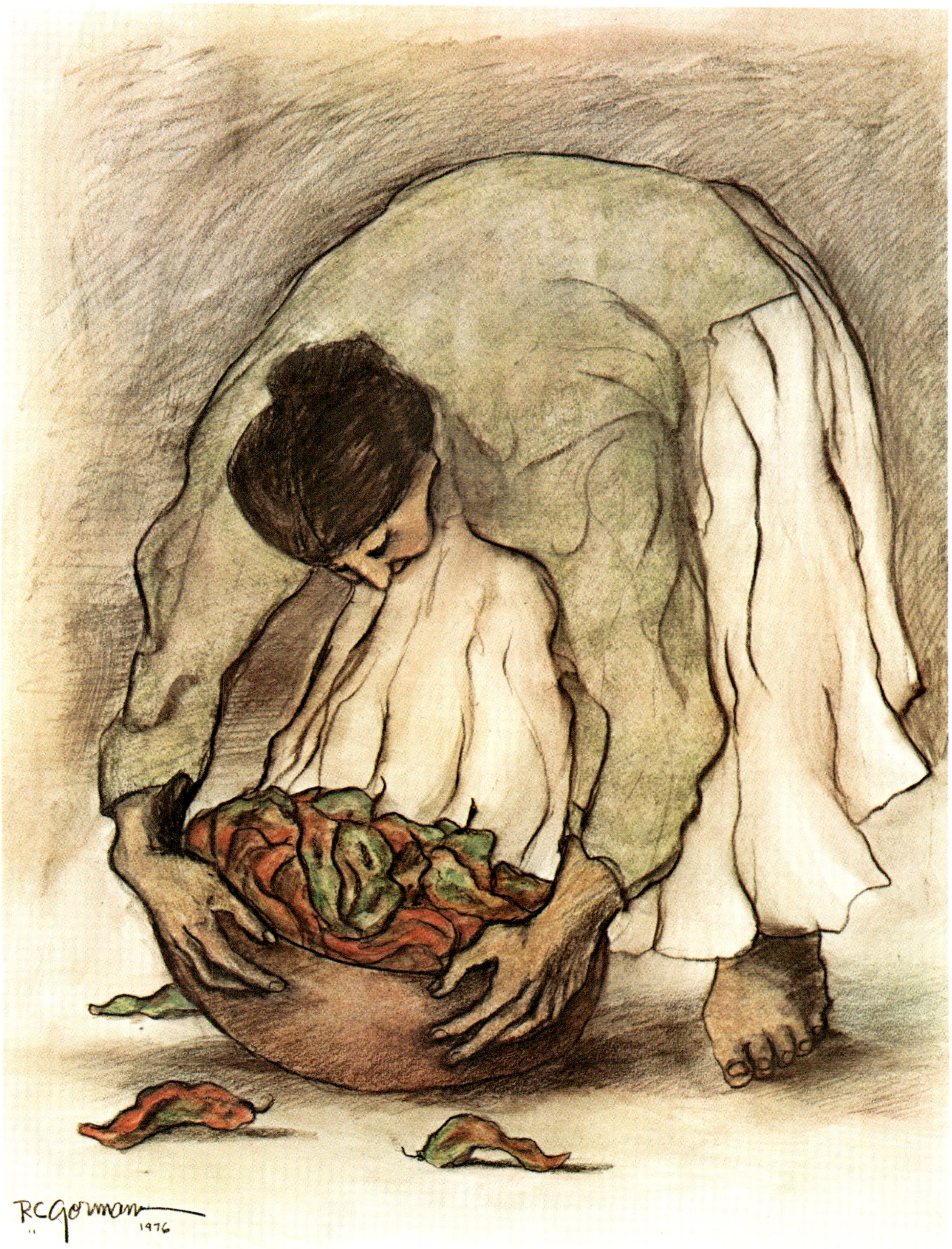

Woman with Chili

from the private collection of Julian Garcia

Rutherford

Paid by Rutherford Campaign Committee, Marilyn O'Leary, Chr. Labor donated by Blue Feather Press.

All Proceeds to benefit the campaign of Tom Rutherford for Lieutenant Governor

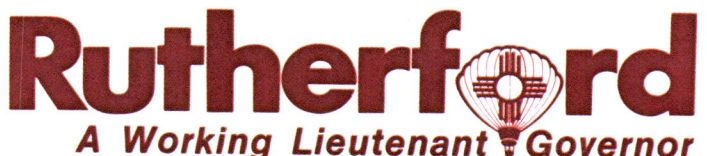

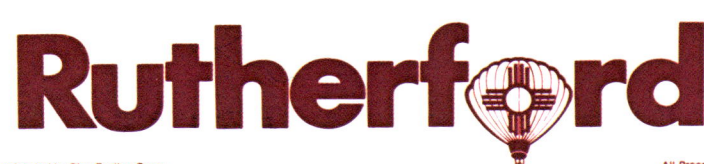

WOMAN WITH CHILI
1976   25 x 17½ inches
Tom Rutherford

YEIBECHEI
1975   30 x 22 inches
Museum of the American Indian, New York City

WOMAN KNEELING
1977   17 x 12 inches
Stables Gallery, Taos

R. C. GORMAN

1978

YOSIE — THE SQUASH BLOSSOM
1978   22½ x 20 inches
White Buffalo Gallery, Wichita

TAOS MAN
1977   31 x 21½ inches
Marjorie Kauffman Graphics, Houston

PORTRAIT OF ANGELINA
1976   22 x 17½ inches
Gallery of New Mexico, Santa Fe

WOMAN WITH ORANGE STRIPED BLANKET
1978   29 x 25 inches
Muirhead Galleries, Ltd., Costa Mesa

SUE-BAH
1978   28 x 22 inches
Suzanne Brown Gallery
(formerly the Art Wagon Gallery), Scottsdale

NIGHT
1978   23½ x 17 inches
Clark-Benton Gallery, Santa Fe

R. C. GORMAN - Navajo Gallery, Taos   1979

LAILA WITH CHILD
1979   24 x 21½ inches
Navajo Gallery, Taos

RECLINING WOMAN
1979   28 x 23 inches
Suzanne Brown Gallery, Scottsdale

WOMAN WITH CLASPED HANDS
1977   23 x 16½ inches
Clark-Benton Gallery, Santa Fe

WOMAN FROM SOUTH DAKOTA
1979   28 x 23 inches
White Buffalo Gallery, Wichita

MOTHER AND CHILD
1978   25 x 18 inches
Suzanne Brown Gallery, Scottsdale

NAVAJO TURQUOISE
1980   28 x 23 inches
Navajo Turquoise Gallery, Paris

R. C. GORMAN

for the Tigua Indians · El Paso, Texas

guynes printing company

TIGUA
1977   25 x 23 inches
R. C. Gorman

Enthios

RCGorman
1977

REPOSING WOMAN
1977   25 x 19 inches
Enthios Gallery, Santa Fe

1976 R.C. GORMAN

WHITE BUFFALO GALLERY

WOMAN WITH RED BELT
1976   25 x 22 inches
White Buffalo Gallery, Wichita

NAVAJO WOMAN WITH PEARS
1977   26 x 21 inches
White Buffalo Gallery, Wichita

LAILA AT REST
1979   23 x 19 inches
White Buffalo Gallery, Wichita

CONTEMPLATION
1977   27½ x 22 inches
Forum del Sol, Albuquerque

RED RIBBON
1979   25½ x 22 inches
Suzanne Brown Gallery, Scottsdale

SUMMER LADY
1978   17 x 10½ inches
Taos Arts Festival, Taos

THREE WOMEN
1979   23 x 19½ inches
Many Horses Gallery, Los Angeles

ZIA
1979   16 x 16 inches
Musée Municipal de Saint-Paul, Saint-Paul de Vence